DR. DROPO'S
BALLOON SCULPTURING
FOR BEGINNERS

BRUCE FIFE, 1952 -

Illustrated by
ED HARRIS

JAVA PUBLISHING CO.
COLORADO SPRINGS

Copyright © 1988, Bruce Fife

All rights reserved. No part of this book may be reproduced in any form without permission in writing from the publisher. Published by Java Publishing Company, 6510 Lehman Drive, Colorado Springs, CO 80918.

Revised Edition

Library of Congress Cataloging-in-Publication Data

Fife, Bruce, 1952-
    Dr. Dropo's balloon sculpturing for beginners / Bruce Fife.
    ISBN 0-941599-01-9
    1. Balloon sculpture. I. Title.
TT926.F54 1988
745.594—dc19   87-36151
                                                  CIP

CONTENTS

INTRODUCTION

My name is Bruce Fife. My friends call me Dr. Dropo. I'm a clown, a juggler, and a professor of balloonology. I teach classes in balloon science and other clown skills as well as demonstrate my balloon sculpturing abilities for countless children.

Being a clown balloonologist, I have the opportunity to make many balloon animals, especially at birthday parties. Balloons and parties go together like ice cream and cake. In my opinion, a party is not complete unless it has balloons, particularly sculptured balloons. These colorful bubbles create a festive atmosphere, provide a fun party activity, and make excellent gifts.

I began to learn the art of balloon sculpturing several years ago when I started performing as "Dr. Dropo" at children's parties. I found that kids go wild over balloon animals and other balloon creations. Taking a limp, lifeless balloon and magically transforming it into a lovable, bubbly animal fascinates and delights children (and even adults).

My own three kids eagerly crowd around me every time I pull out a balloon. I'll make them each several figures. Then, with arms filled to capacity, they'll scamper off to their rooms, deposit their treasure, and race back for more. Do they ever get tired of them? Not in the least. Over the years I've made hundreds of the cute little creatures and still their eyes light up with excitement every time they see me with a balloon.

This book was written for those who would like to share in the excitement of balloon sculpturing, experience the thrill of turning a skinny piece of rubber into a cute, lovable animal, and put smiles on children's faces (and on their own).

I have designed this book to teach beginners the basics of balloon sculpturing, using easy-to-follow directions supplemented by clear illustrations to guide you every step of the way. The figures I've selected for this book include the ever-popular dog, as well as rabbits, frogs, bugs, funny hats, and even games and toys. Although I can't claim all of the figures in this book to be my own original creations, all of the figures are favorites with kids and easy enough for any beginner to master with only a few minutes of practice.

CHAPTER 1

BALLOON BASICS

Like people, balloons come in all sizes and shapes. To make figures from a single balloon you will need special balloons known as *pencil balloons* or *twistys*. These skinny balloons grow very long when inflated, allowing the sculptor to twist them into an endless variety of shapes.

The most popular balloons used for modeling are #260A and #260E pencil balloons. The "2" in the code "260" refers to the diameter of the balloon in inches when it's fully inflated. The "60" designates the length of the inflated balloon. The "A" stands for average strength and the "E" for entertainer grade. The thicker-walled #260E balloons are a little harder to inflate, but can withstand more twisting and pulling. Most of the figures in this book can be made with either the #260A or the #260E. Other balloons that are used less frequently are #245 and the *apple* and the *bee body* (#321).

These balloons can be obtained at novelty stores, such as magic shops, and by mail order. Sometimes they can be found in toy stores.

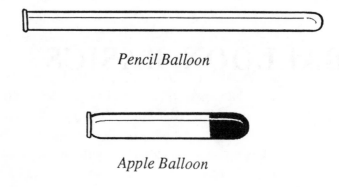

Pencil Balloon

Apple Balloon

BALLOON CARE

In order to avoid unnecessary blowouts and to keep your balloon in good working order, you need to know about proper balloon maintenance.

Very little care is needed to keep your balloons in good working order. They never need washing or ironing; they need no food, oil, or periodic checkups. Being made of latex, however, balloons are perishable and will deteriorate with age. Heat, sunlight, and air are the balloon's worst enemies. If you keep the balloons out of the sunlight in an airtight container, and store them in a cool place they should remain usable for a year or more. Students have come to my balloon sculpturing clasess with balloons over two years old, and they had no problems. But if you buy a package of balloons and leave them on the dashboard of your car on a hot summer day, don't expect them to last more than a day or so.

If you plan to store your balloons for a while, sprinkle a little cornstarch or talcum powder on them. This prevents them from becoming sticky with age and prolongs their life.

With proper care and storage, balloons will last a long time. Storing them in a freezer or refrigerator normally isn't necessary.

As you work with balloons you will find, even with a fresh package of balloons, some variation in quality. Every package of balloons I've ever used have had its share of duds—balloons with tiny holes or thin spots that break when inflated. This is to be expected with any package of pencil balloons you buy, so don't be surprised to find a few bad ones.

INFLATION

All new balloon sculptors are surprised at the difficulty of inflating pencil balloons. Because the balloons' diameter is so small, blowing them up takes a good set of lungs.

To soften the balloon and make it easier to inflate, stretch it a few times. But be careful not to overstretch it; a balloon stretched to its limits will develop lumps when inflated.

To inflate the balloon, use your cheek muscles to start a bubble. Once the bubble is started, take a deep breath and use your chest and diaphragm muscles to inflate the rest of the balloon with one continuous blow.

Some people like to pull the nipple end of the balloon as

they blow. This action tends to encourage the air into the balloon, making inflation somewhat easier. If you try this, don't be overzealous. If you pull too much or too fast, you'll make inflation more difficult.

When you first try to inflate the skinny #260 balloons, you may even experience some dizziness. But with a week or two of light practice your lung strength should increase and you will no longer be troubled with this feeling.

If after stretching the balloon and you still have trouble inflating it, don't give up; there's another method that makes putting air in a balloon as easy as tooting on a whistle. The secret? An air pump. That's right—almost any hand pump can be used, as long as the nozzle of the balloon can fit on it. I used a ordinary foot pump when I started as a balloon sculptor. Pumps can be purchased at stores that sell bicycles or sporting goods. Hand pumps designed specially for balloons are also available. These can be obtained in local novelty shops or by mail order. Another advantage to using a pump is that you can inflate a limitless number of balloons without killing yourself. For a clown surrounded by a mob of kids anxiously waiting for each creation, a pump comes in mighty handy. How much air should you put into the balloon? Rarely will you ever inflate it fully. Leave an inch or two uninflated at the very end. As you tie off the balloon and begin to twist bubbles, the remaining air will be forced toward the end, gradually inflating the tail. If you don't leave this tail, the end of the balloon will stretch tighter and tighter, making it difficult to twist the bubbles and increasing the chances of popping.

The type of animal you make determines how long this tail should be. A dog, for instance, needs only two inches uninflated. A mouse needs six or seven inches.

Balloon Busting

Sometimes when you blow up a balloon, that's exactly what happens—it blows up! I've noticed an inherent fear of blowouts, especially in beginners. They twist the bubbles very gingerly, as if expecting them to explode at any second. Some clench their teeth tightly, as if that would prevent the balloon from popping. Others close their eyes, tense up, and contort their faces, stretching them more than the balloon. I even find myself doing this at times. But never, never, never, in all the time I have been working with balloons and in all the classes I've taught, never has anybody ever been mortally wounded by a popped balloon.

I have yet to see a drop of blood, a dislocated shoulder, a blister, a bruise, or any other physical injury caused by such a mishap.

Exploding balloons are a part of the balloon sculptor's experience. Like taxes, there is no way around them. You can be as careful as a nitroglycerine salesman, but all balloons are not made equal. Some will pop without apparent reason, no matter how careful you are. I've been hit in the face only once, that I can recall, with a piece of exploding balloon. It left no disfiguring scar and I lived to tell about it, so don't worry about popping your bubbles.

Most pencil balloons are surprisingly resilient, especially the #260E variety. They can withstand a lot of twisting, tugging, stretching, and shoving without breaking.

To cut down on the number of balloons that will pop and to make the balloons easier to work with, I recommend that you treat them like a little baby after it's had a meal. I don't mean change its diaper—but to "burp it." Before tying off the end, let out a little air, just enough to make it "burp." This will make the balloon softer and easier to work with.

Tying Off the Balloon

There are several ways to tie off a balloon. Any method that works is acceptable. I have two methods I like best. Experiment with both and see what one you prefer, or use a method of your own.

First Method. Hold the balloon between the thumb and first finger of one hand, as shown in the illustration below. With the other hand pull the nozzle down and around the first finger. Tuck the nozzle under the loop and pull it through.

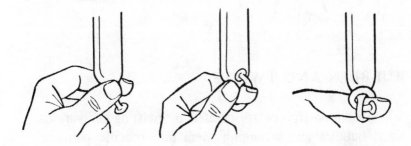

14

Second Method. This method works well for those who have thin fingers. My fingers are on the thin side, so I usually tie my balloons this way.

Start by holding the balloon between the thumb and first finger, as shown below. Wrap the nozzle around the ends of the first two fingers. Insert the nozzle under the loop. Pull on the nozzle, making a knot while slipping your fingers out.

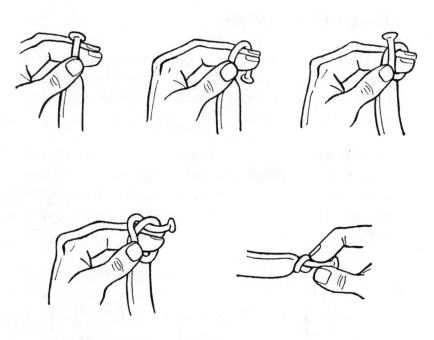

BUBBLES AND TWISTS

Balloon figures are created by twisting off various sized bubbles and arranging them into specific patterns. The bubbles are made by twisting the balloon in opposite directions. Twist each bubble at least two complete revolutions so they won't unravel as you work.

Four basic types of bubbles are commonly used: small, medium, large, and extra large.

I define small bubbles as those that have a smaller diameter than the diameter of the rest of the balloon. This size bubble is commonly used for ears and noses.

Medium bubbles have a diameter equal to that of the rest of the balloon. Ears, necks, and small legs are made from these bubbles.

16

Large bubbles have a length slightly longer than the balloon's diameter. These bubbles are good for legs, long ears, and arms.

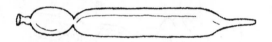

Extra large bubbles include all those which are longer than the large bubbles. This type of bubble is commonly used to make bodies of figures and long legs.

After twisting off these bubbles, make sure you continue to hold them, or they will untwist. Only after you have made an connecting twist can you let go. Connecting twists are usually used to connect two or more bubbles.

As an example, twist out three medium sized bubbles (1, 2, and 3).

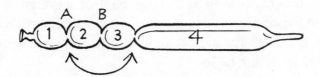

Make sure you twist each bubble in the same direction or they will untwist in your hand. Connect point A with point B (see illustration). While holding bubbles 4 and 1, twist together bubbles 3 and 2 as shown below.

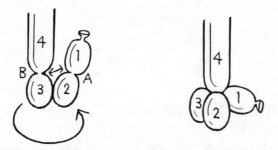

This is the basic type of twist that you'll use to make connections. Another type of connecting twist, called a *loop twist*, is also important. A loop twist is simply a bubble connected to itself (see illustration).

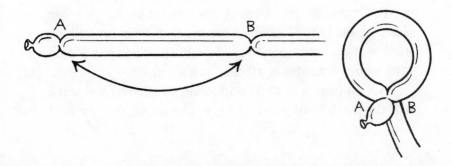

Loop twists with extra large bubbles make good hats. Loop twisting small and medium sized bubbles make good ears or wings for animal figures, and sometimes are referred to as *ear twists*.

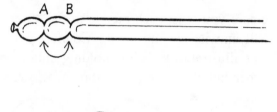

CHARACTER AIDS

Markings such as mouth and eyes can give your creation a personality, thus making it more realistic. Most all figures you make will take on a more recognizable and lifelike appearance with the addition of these character aids. Certain animals may require distinguishing marks such as whiskers, spots, and stripes to make them recognizable.

Markings can do wonders in bringing your figure to life, but don't overdo it! Usually the fewest marks you can make are the best. Too much ink distracts from the balloon itself, and can even look ugly. For most figures just adding eyes and/or a mouth is all that is needed.

Not all pens will write on the latex balloons, and some that do, don't look good. I have discovered that the best

type of pen is a permanent felt tip marker such as Sanford's Sharpie. These pens give a nice solid black line that I can make either fat or thin, depending on how I use it.

Balloons come in a variety of colors, adding to the character of each creation. Although figures can be made in any color, some animals look better when made with certain colors. A swan looks best if made with a white balloon; a bee is more recognizable if you use a yellow balloon; a ladybug looks best in red or orange.

The fact that you can make most figures out of any color adds variety to your creations. Even if you can make only two or three different animals, each creation can be unique when you use different colors and make different markings and expressions.

CHAPTER 2

BALLOON ANIMALS

Let's start with the easiest and most popular balloon creature—the annelid. What's an annelid? You'll recognize it when you're finished.

Inflate a balloon about a foot or so and tie it off (the exact amount of air for this creature is not important). Now take a pin or a ballpoint pen and make a hole, popping the balloon. You will be left with a long, scrawny piece of rubber which resembles an annelid. (If you don't recognize what an annelid is, it's a worm!)

Worms aren't that popular with kids, but balloonologists love to make them—they make them all time, almost as if by accident.

There's an endless variety of methods for making worms. Some are very complex, involving many bubbles and twists before popping, but the end result is always the same—the worm.

As a new balloonologist, you too will learn to master the worm, and it will soon become one of your most often repeated creations.

Now that I've discussed one of the unavoidable mishaps of balloon sculpturing, let's look at some serious creations.

THE BASIC DOG

The dog is a basic balloon figure. It's easy to make, and is requested most often by children. Once you have learned how to make the basic dog, making many of the other balloon animals will be easy.

To make the dog, start by inflating a pencil balloon all the way to the end except for about two or three inches. "Burp" it to let a little bit of air escape, and then tie off the nozzle end. Twist off three large bubbles (1, 2, and 3) each about three inches long, and twist connect them at points A and B.

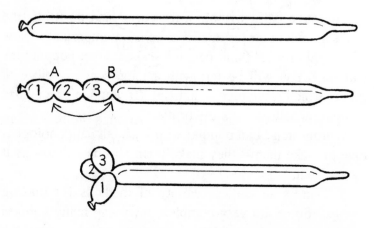

Twist off three more bubbles of the same size (4, 5, and 6) and connect points C and D.

Make an extra large bubble (7) for the body and twist off two additional large bubbles (8 and 9) the same size as bubbles 5 and 6. You will be left with only a small bubble (10) at the end, to be used as the tail.

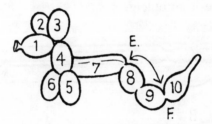

Twist connect points E and F. Arrange the bubbles in a realistic position and finish by marking in eyes and mouth.

The steps used to make the dog are basically the same for many other types of animals. By varying the size of the bubbles on the dog's body, you can create other animals. Let's take a look at some of these animals.

DACHSHUND

As far as hounds are concerned the dachshund is a low down dog. But it makes a good family dog because all the members of the family can pat it at the same time.

The sequence for making the dachshund is the same as that just described for the dog. The only difference is that you lengthen the body and shorten the legs slightly.

Connect the bubbles as shown below. Draw in eyes and mouth to make it complete.

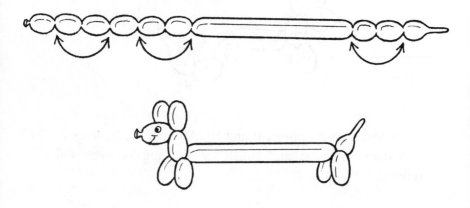

GIRAFFE

What do giraffes have that no other animal has . . . ? Little giraffes of course.

The giraffe is made by lengthening the neck on the basic

dog figure. The legs are also lengthened and the ears are shortened. The addition of semi-square spots on the neck makes the giraffe easily recognizable.

MOUSE

The mouse is one of my favorite balloon animals. It's quick and easy to make, and kids love it.

The mouse's head is almost as large as the dog's, but the rest of the bubbles are smaller. Since the bubbles are small, the balloon should be inflated no more than 12 inches. This will leave a long uninflated portion of the balloon at the nipple end, which will become the the mouse's tail.

Twist off a medium to large bubble to form the head. All other bubbles except the body will be medium. The body will be a large bubble. Draw in eyes, mouth and whiskers to finish (see the illustrations on the next page).

SQUIRREL

I'm nutty about this animal, but my friends tell me I'm just nutty.

The squirrel is made with medium sized bubbles, just like the mouse. The only difference is the tail; for the squirrel it's fully inflated.

Begin by inflating a balloon fully except for about two inches. Twist off and connect the bubble just as you do with the mouse.

Shaping the tail helps to make the squirrel lifelik To put a permanent curve in the balloon, bend it in the direction you want it to curve and squeeze the sides a couple of times. The tail will retain a squirrel-like curve. For the final touch, add a squirrel face like the one pictured here.

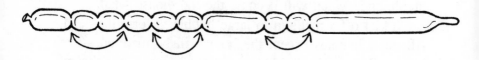

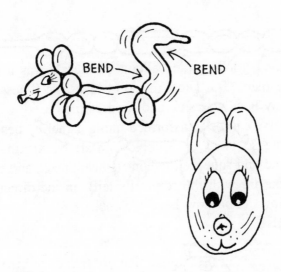

HORSE

The horse, the original oatsmobile, will have slightly longer legs and neck than the dog. The ears should be made from small bubbles. Marking a mane on the back of the horse's neck helps distinguish it from the dog.

CAMEL

Before I got into the balloon business I was a used camel salesman. But I lost my job because of illness and fatigue—my boss was sick and tired of me.

The horse can be transformed into a camel by bending and shaping some of the bubbles. Start by making the horse. Bend and squeeze the horse's head, neck, and body (just as you did with the squirrel's tail) in the directions shown below. You now have a camel.

KANGAROO

The kangaroo is made much like the horse, except that the front legs are short. Leave about five or six inches of the balloon uninflated. This will give the finished figure a long, kangaroo-type tail.

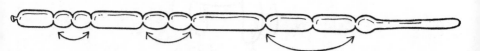

POODLE

The poodle is much like the basic dog figure, with some notable differences. The neck is shorter and the legs are longer. Inflate the balloon fully except for about four inches. Twist off the bubbles and connect them as you would the basic dog.

After you finish making all the bubbles and all the connecting twists, two additional manipulations give this figure its distinctive poodle appearance. Take bubble 1 and push it a fourth of the way between bubbles 2 and 3. This gives the figure poodle-type ears.

With one hand hold bubble 10 and half of the uninflated portion of the tail. With the other hand grab the tip of the tail and stretch it by pulling it several times. This stretching will weaken the end of the balloon so air can form a bubble there without inflating the rest of the tail.

Hold bubble 10 and the unstretched portion of the tail and squeeze. A bubble should develop at the end of the tail.

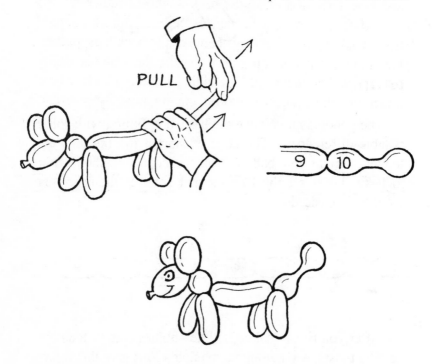

Another way to make this bubble is to put the end of the uninflated tail in your mouth and suck the air into that part of the balloon. A small bubble will develop in your mouth, and your tail is finished. Some people prefer this method over the first one, but it leaves your poodle's tail wet and a rubbery taste in your mouth.

RABBIT

I learned how to make these rabbits at my last job, where I worked as a rabbit breeder—it really kept me hopping.

To create a rabbit, give the basic dog figure longer ears and hind legs, and make the neck slightly smaller.

After twisting off all bubbles and making all connections, push the two front legs between the back legs, putting the rabbit into a sitting position. Usually the rabbit is easily recognizable at this stage, but adding a bunny like face (use a face like the squirrel's) it turns into a cute, bubbly rabbit.

How can you find a lost rabbit? Simple, just make a noise like a carrot.

FROG

"Burlap!". . . Excuse me. Every time I make this figure I get a frog in my throat.

The frog is made in much the same way as the rabbit,

with some notable differences. The first four bubbles combine to form the frog's head.

Inflate the balloon fully except for about two inches. Bubble 1 is a medium bubble. Bubbles 2 and 3 are the frog's eyes, and bubble 4 is its mouth. There is no neck bubble in this figure.

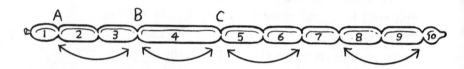

Twist off the first three bubbles and connect points A and B. Twist off bubble 4 and make a loop twist, connecting points B and C.

Push bubbles 1, 2, and 3 up through the center of bubble 4 to create the frog's head (see the illustration below).

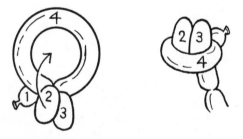

Twist off and connect the rest of the bubbles and tuck the two front legs between the back legs, as you did for the rabbit. Adding a face to the frog makes it easily recognizable.

MUGWUMP

"What's a mugwump?" you ask. A mugwump is an animal that sits on a fence with its mug on one side and its wump on the other.

Since this is an imaginary creature, you can make it look like most anything you want. This is my version.

Inflate a pencil balloon, leaving two inches uninflated. Follow the steps for making the standard dog figure, using a four-inch long bubble for the nose, and leave a long, squirrel-type tail. I also make the front legs shorter than the back ones. Put a bend in the nose and tail, as shown, and draw in a face.

Although the mugwump doesn't represent any real animal that I know of, kids enjoy it because it's cute.

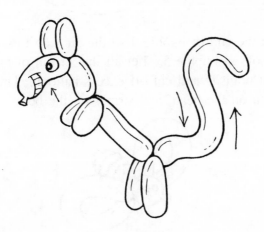

BUMBLEBEE

We now depart from the basic dog figure and begin making figures which have different shapes. Several winged creations can be made using just four bubbles.

The bumblebee is a simple little balloon figure kids adore. For appearance's sake a yellow balloon works best. Inflate the balloon at least 18 inches, leaving a long, uninflated tail. Bubble 1, which is the bee's head, is medium sized. Bubbles 2 and 3, which are the wings, are extra large bubbles about six or seven inches long. Bubble 4 is another extra large bubble, but only three inches long.

Make bubbles 1 and 2 first. Loop twist bubble 2 by connecting points A and B. Now twist off bubble 3 and loop twist it, connecting points B and C. Twist off bubble 4, which will become the bee's body.

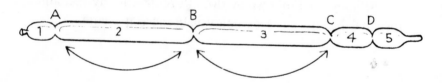

Hold the end of bubble 4 so the air won't escape and make a hole in bubble 5. Let all the air out of bubble 5. Tie off at point D and cut off excess balloon. Draw eyes and mouth on the head, and stripes on the body.

HUMMINGBIRD

Some birds sing, others whistle, but a hummingbird hums—why is that. . . ? Because he doesn't know the words.

The hummingbird is made in much the same way as the bee. Inflate the balloon fully, leaving a two-inch tail. For this figure you work backward, stararing at the nipple end and work toward the nozzle.

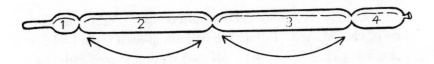

Twist off a medium to large bubble, leaving the nipple for the bird's long beak. Twist off bubbles 2 and 3, loop connecting each one in turn. The remaining bubble becomes the hummingbird's body.

LADYBUG

Flying insects bug some people more than others. Some people shoo them, while others just let them run around barefoot.

The ladybug is one of the cutest little balloon figures I've ever seen. Although it takes only four bubbles, it's a little harder to make than the others you've worked on so far. The tricky part about the ladybug is making the small loop twists (ear twists). These twists get tight, and may take a little practice to master. Ear twists are easier to make if you soften the balloon by releasing a little extra air before tying it off.

Orange, red, and yellow balloons look best, but any color can be used. Inflate the balloon at least eight inches, leaving a long tail. Twist off two medium sized bubbles, a small bubble, and another medium bubble, and hold them.

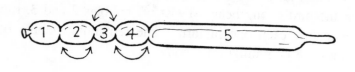

Ear twist bubbles 2, 3, and 4. Twist bubble 3 first, then 2, and finally 4.

Make a small hole in bubble 5 and release the air. This bubble will deflate, but the others will remain airtight. Use a pair of scissors to cut off the deflated portion of the balloon.

Arrange the bubbles to look like the figure below. Bubble 1 becomes the body, bubble 3 the head, and bubbles 2 and 4 the wings. Add spots to the bug's back and draw in a face.

SWAN

What did the swan say when it laid a square egg?
"Ouch!"

The swan is one of the classic balloon figures most all balloon sculptors have in their repertoire. Its long slender neck and simple twists make it ideal for balloon sculpturing. Many versions exist, but the one I show you here is my favorite.

Inflate a pencil balloon fully except for three or four inches. Make a medium bubble (1), followed by two extra large bubbles (2 and 3). Connect the bubbles at points A and B.

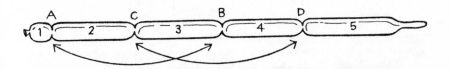

Twist off bubble 4. Bubbles 2, 3, and 4 should all be the same length. Connect points C and D by simply pushing on top of point D. You don't need to make any twists for this connection (see illustration).

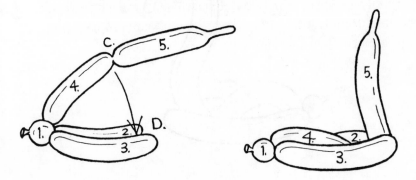

The remaining bubble will become the swan's head and neck. Making the head requires a trick that may take a little practice. Bend the nipple over and grab the balloon about an inch below the top, as shown in the illustration. Grabbing the neck of the balloon with both hands, squeeze tightly, forcing air up into the tip. For best results, squeeze only once but squeeze hard.

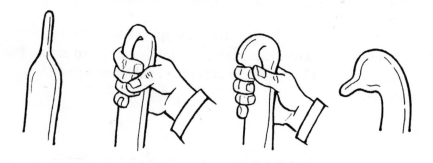

Bend and shape the swan's neck into a natural curve. A pair of eyes is all the marking you need to finish this figure.

SEAL BALANCING A BALL

This is a seal-ly (silly) balloon figure that you're sure to enjoy.

The seal is made very much like the swan. Inflate the balloon, leaving three or four inches in the tail. Twist off bubbles 1, 2, 3, and 4 and connect them as shown, just as if you're making the swan's body.

Twist off medium sized bubbles 5 and 6 and connect as shown to form the front fins. To make the ball on the seal's nose, follow the same procedure as you did when making the poodle's tail. Stretch the tip of the uninflated portion of bubble 7 and then squeeze the bubble, forcing air into the tip. You'll end up with a small bubble joined by a short section of uninflated balloon, which looks like a ball on the seal's nose.

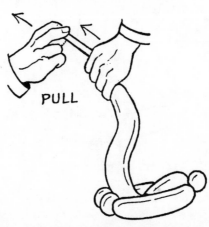

PULL

Finish by shaping the seal's neck into the proper position.

Put your seal of approval on this one by clapping your hands and say "Arf."

CHAPTER 3

APPLE BALLOONS

Apple balloons are much shorter than pencil balloons and a bit wider, so they're easier to inflate. They come in a variety of colors, most commonly red, yellow, green, and light blue. Their most distinguishing characteristic is the dark green nipple, which forms the stem when making the apple.

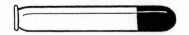

APPLE

Use a short apple balloon to make this classic. Inflate the balloon about halfway. With your finger push the nozzle into the balloon and all the way into the nipple end. Grab both the nipple and the nozzle with the fingers of your other hand and remove your finger. Now make an *apple twist* by turning the bubble as you hold the two ends securely. This action will lock the nozzle and nipple together forming an apple-shaped bubble.

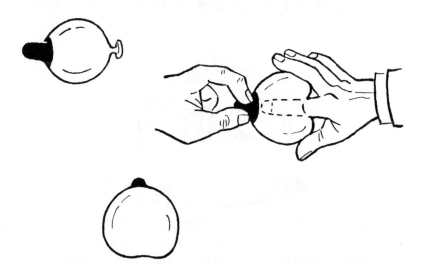

You can make different types of apples by changing the color: red apples, green and yellow apples, and even blue apples.

BASKET OF FRUIT

A basket of fruit can be created by making an assortment of red, green, and yellow apples, combined with bananas and grapes.

The bananas are made from yellow pencil balloons. Use only eight or nine inches of the balloon and put a banana-like curve in it.

The grapes are made from red, yellow, or purple pencil balloons. Inflate the balloon and twist off a bunch of small bubbles. Connect the bubbles to form a bunch of grapes.

Put all the balloon fruit in a basket or bowl, and you have a decorative arrangement. Anyone care for a snack?

BUBBLE BABY

Apple balloons were produced originally to make rubber apples, but they can easily be transformed into bubble babies and balloon guys. Many variations are possible; here are a few to get you started.

Making the bubble baby and all the other balloon guys is very similar to making the rubber apple. The major difference is that you don't push the nozzle all the way up to the nipple.

To make the bubble baby, inflate an apple balloon about halfway and tie it off. Push the nozzle up inside the balloon and over to one side in the *lower half* of the balloon. Grab the knot from the outside with the other hand and remove your finger from the inside of the balloon (see illustration).

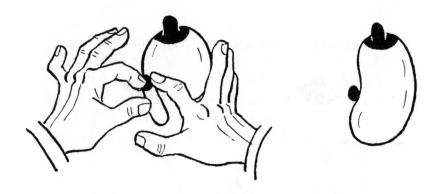

Twist the knot to form a little knob in the center of the balloon. This knob becomes the baby's nose. The natural bend in the bubble makes the cheeks, and a fold forms the mouth. To finish, all you need to do is draw in a pair of eyes.

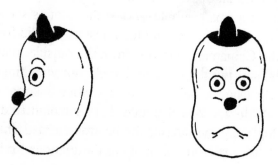

CHINAMAN

The Chinaman is made in exactly the same way as the baby except that the knot is pushed up and connected to the *upper half* of the balloon. Twisting off the nose closer to the top of the head creates a more adult-shaped head and more pronounced folds in the balloon, giving its distinct appearance.

Mark eyes as shown, and you're finished.

BALDHEADED MAN

Inflate an apple balloon about halfway and tie it off. Twist off a small bubble next to the knot as shown below. Push the knot and the bubble up just as you did for the baby and the Chinaman. Grab it from the outside, remove your finger, and twist it off (the bubble not your finger).

By using a bubble you give your balloon guy a big bulbous nose. You'll notice that a mouth fold does not develop this time. Also, the head stretches, removing the dimple on top of it and making the green color blend into the rest of the balloon.

Draw in eyes and a mouth.

BUBBLES THE CLOWN

The clown is the same as the baldheaded man except that clown markings are added.

MR. MUSTACHE

Mr. Mustache is made much like the bubble baby except that you use a penny or a small marble to form the nose. Inflate an apple balloon as before. Place a penny on the knot and push both the penny and the knot inside the balloon. With the other hand grab the penny and the knot from the outside on the *lower half* of the balloon, remove the inside finger, and twist the penny to connect.

Your figure will have a large, but flat nose with several wrinkles under it, which look like whiskers. There will be no mouth fold, so you must draw the mouth in. Mark in the eyes and darken the mustache.

TROLL

This little creature is so gruesome that he's cute.

Begin the troll as you did Mr. Mustache, with a half inflated balloon and a penny. Push the penny and the knot inside the balloon, grabbing them from the outside with the other hand on the *upper half* of the balloon near where the green color begins. Twist to connect and form the nose.

Making the nose this far up the balloon forms a pronounced bend that produces many folds, including a frowning mouth fold. The nipple on top of the head moves down to the figure's forehead, forming a horn.

The addition of beady eyes and perhaps fangs, is all that's needed to complete this troll figure. Adorable! The kids will squeal . . . with delight.

ZIGGY

If you enjoy the cartoon character Ziggy, you'll like this Ziggy look-alike figure.

Inflate an apple balloon about one-third this time, and tie it off. You need less air so you can form a more rounded head.

Use a penny or a marble and push it all the way up *into the nipple.* As you do this, curve the balloon slightly to one side so you don't end up making an apple. Twist to make the nose.

Position the mouth fold so that it's at the bottom of the balloon. Draw in the eyes and add a smile.

MR. WRINKLE

Inflate an apple balloon halfway and tie it off. By using a penny you can give the nose a remarkably human shape. This is done by not pushing the penny all the way to the end of the nipple, thus trapping a small pocket of air. Try this with Mr. Wrinkle.

As you push the penny inside the balloon, bring the mouth fold close to the nose before twisting. This will stretch the back side of the head but will bunch the face, giving Mr. Wrinkle his wrinkles.

Draw on a pair of squinty eyes, and he's finished.

THE MASKED MARVEL

The Masked Marvel is the superhero of the balloon guys. Like all good superheros he wears a mask to hide his true identity.

You'll notice that the amount of green on the balloons varies from one balloon to the next; some balloons having more than others. In order to make the Masked Marvel you need to use a balloon with a substantial amount of green; this is what makes his mask. Use yellow and blue balloons because they seem to keep the color contrast during stretching better than the other colors.

If the balloon you're using has a large amount of green, you can insert the penny all the way to the tip of the nipple before twisting it off. If it has only a moderate amout of green you may position the penny on the side of the nipple rather than in the tip.

Twist to form the nose. A mouth fold should be present, so all you need to do is add eyes in the figure's "mask".

MORE BALLOON GUYS

A number of other faces can be made by varying the amount of air put into the balloon and the type of nose used. Chin size can be adjusted by moving the mouth closer or farther away from the nose before making the connecting twist. And of course, the markings you add can do a lot for creating character. Experiment and see what types of balloon guys you can create.

A toy that has become popular with children during the past few years is the Mad Ball, a rubber ball with a grotesque face. They're extremely ugly—I guess that's why they're popular. With the stroke of your pen it's an easy task to transform a balloon guy into a horrible-looking Mad Ball, or more accurately a Mad Ball-oon.

CHAPTER 4

BALLOON HATS

BASIC BALLOON HAT

Balloon hats are easy to make and popular with kids. I'll describe how to make a basic hat and use that as the starting point for making a variety of styles.

Inflate a pencil balloon fully except for about two inches. Twist off a medium bubble. To determine the size of bubble 2, wrap the rest of the balloon around the head the intended recipient. Remove the balloon and loop twist bubble 2, connecting points A and B.

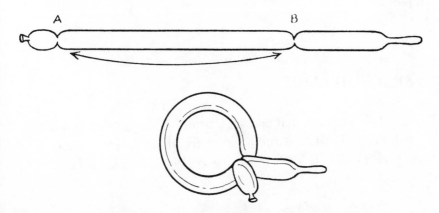

The basic hat is now complete. With bubble 3 sticking up in back it looks like an Indian headband and feather. Put this hat on your head—it will keep your "wig-wam".

Turning the Indian hat upside down transforms it into a coonskin balloon cap. Add another balloon and you can make a variety of hats, such as the space helmet described below.

SPACE HELMET

Make the basic hat and set it aside. Take another pencil balloon and inflate it fully except for about an inch. Starting at the nozzle end, make the connections shown here.

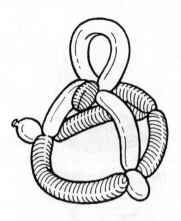

To make the antenna, squeeze the loop on top of the hat and twist it in half as shown. You're now finished.

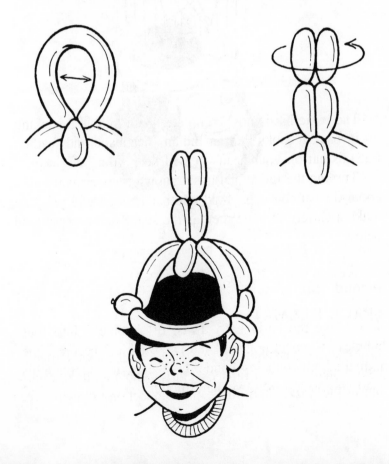

ANIMAL HATS

First Hat

Make the basic balloon hat. With bubble 3 make a bird's head and beak in the same way you would make the swan's head. Finish by adding eyes.

Second Hat

Make the basic hat. Twist off bubble 3 into four bubbles. Connect points C and D. Bubble 3 becomes the animal's body, bubbles 4 and 5 his wings, and bubble 6 his head and nose. Add eyes and mouth.

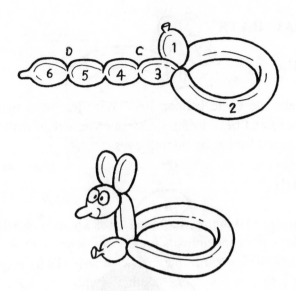

Third Hat

This hat is made much like the previous one. From the basic hat take bubble 3 and squeeze the air down to eliminate the tail. Leave only a small nipple. This will make the balloon soft.

Make bubbles 3, 4, 5, and 6. Loop twist bubble 4 by connecting points C and D. Make a second loop twist around bubble 5 by connecting points D and E. This forms two ears. Bubble 6 becomes the animal's head. Add eyes and mouth.

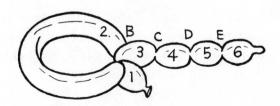

Fourth Hat

Start by making the basic hat. Take a second balloon and make any of the animals previously described (or even the airplane described in the next chapter). Twist connect the figure to the top of the "feather" bubble.

CHAPTER 5

GAMES AND TOYS

AIRPLANE

If an athlete gets athlete's foot, what do astronauts get? You guessed it—missile toe.

This fun toy balloon looks like the old doubled wing biplane of World War I. To make an airplane, inflate a balloon fully except for about two inches. Twist off one large bubble, about two and a half inches long, this will be the plane's nose. Twist off two extra large bubbles (2 and 3) making them about four inches long. Connect points A and B.

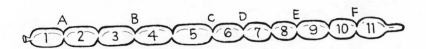

Twist off bubbles 4 and 5, making sure that they are the same size as bubbles 2 and 3. Connect points B and C.

You're finished with the plane's front wings, now twist off a large bubble (6) to form the central body segment.

Twist off two three-inch long bubbles (7 and 8) and connect them at points D and E for one pair of rear wings. Do the same with bubbles 9 and 10 to finish the figure.

One last step makes the airplane easily recognizable and realistic—adding a propeller. To do this take a wooden match and break off and discard the matchhead. Keep the length of the match at least one and a half inches long. Now insert the match inside the rim of the nozzle.

Push the match through the rubber so that the rubber splits open just behind the outside rim. Make a hole on the other side and center the match. Your propeller is now in place, and your plane is finished. Now take the plane and buzz off!

HIGH-FLYERS

Although the airplane just described can't fly on its own power, here are some balloons that can.

Inflate a pencil balloon fully without tying it off and ask, "What's this balloon going to be?" After listening to all the responses say, "Nope!" Release the balloon letting it fly around the room, "It's a shooting star."

Flying balloons always excite kids—they even excite me (I guess that means I'm really just an overgrown kid). Everyone will want to fly these balloons themselves. It makes a fun activity.

Bubble Rocket Ship

A small bubble rocket ship can be made using four bubbles. To make the bubble ship, inflate a pencil balloon fully, leaving only a small dimple at the end. This will become the ship's nose. Let a little of the air back out to soften the balloon. Keep hold of the nozzle, without tying it off (you may have to pinch it closed by stepping on it).

At the nipple end twist off one medium to large-sized bubble (1) and three small bubbles (2, 3, and 4). Ear twist bubbles 2, 3, and 4. Position the three bubbles (boosters) evenly around the base of bubble 1.

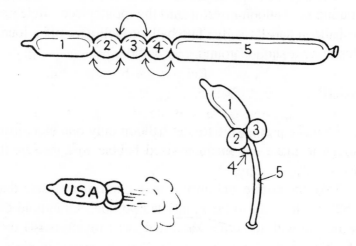

Your bubble rocket ship is now ready. Fuel up by re-inflating the balloon if necessary. Aim, release, and watch it soar.

Spinner

A spinner can be made by curling the balloon as you inflate it or by bending and shaping it after you've put in the air. When released, it will twirl in the air—a dazzling sight!

Whistling Flyer

Cut a piece of stiff cardboard about ¹/₂" x ³/₄". After inflating the balloon insert it into the mouthpiece. Release the balloon and let it fly. The balloon will give off a loud whistle as it shoots around the room.

TULIP

To make a tulip, inflate the balloon only one inch, just enough to make one medium-sized bubble, and then tie it off.

Take the nozzle and push it with one finger, inside the bubble all the way to the uninflated portion. Grab hold of the nozzle with the other hand and twist (apple twist) the bubble a couple of revolutions, locking the nozzle in place.

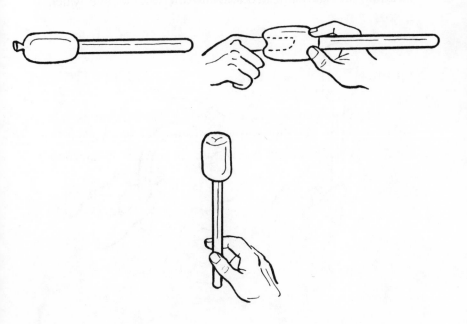

The tulip is now complete. Using different colored balloons you can make several, put them in a vase and have a bouquet. These flowers require very little care and never dry up or turn brown, although they will wilt after a few days.

The Wilting Tulip

A tulip can be used as a fun game with kids. Tell everyone that the flower you created is magic, and can "smell." Its sense of smell is so good that it can identify those who ate fish-flavored Jello for lunch.

Hold the tulip with your thumb and first finger. Ask someone to blow on the flower. As he does so, pinch the stem lightly and push the thumb gently upward, making the movement as inconspicuous as possible. When you do this the flower will drop over, as if dead. Claim that the person must have eaten fish-flavored Jello for lunch.

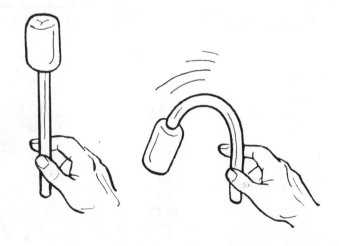

To "revive" the tulip, fan it with your free hand to give it fresh air. Release your grip on the stem slightly and shift the thumb down, allowing the flower to pop back up.

Repeat this stunt with everyone present. Most will want to have their breath tested. Have the tulip wilt each time and claim each of them have been eating fish Jello. You can test it out yourself with the same wilting results, to all the kids delight.

ELEPHANT NOSE

This is more of a gag than a balloon figure, but it's easy to make and gets a quick laugh.

Use a #245 pencil balloon or cut a #260 in half before starting. Inflate a balloon fully, leaving only about one-half inch uninflated.

Twist off two medium-sized bubbles. Ear twist bubble 2. If the balloon doesn't already have a natural curve, put one in by bending it. Now your balloon is complete. Just clamp bubbles 1 and 2 on your nose and you've become an elephant (or Pinocchio). The kids will want to try on this nose for size.

You can make various sized noses depending on the size and shape of the balloon. This is a good way to use a scrap piece of balloon.

Nose Game

Make several of these elephant trunks and have a nosefight. Any number of players can participate, each wearing a balloon nose. The object of the game is to knock the balloon off of the other players' noses using only your elephant nose—no hands allowed. The one who can keep the balloon nose on his or her face the longest is the winner.

CLOWN NOSE

Using a red apple balloon you can make a bulbous clown nose. Inflate the balloon about halfway and twist off two small bubbles, one at each end of the balloon. Pull them together and twist connect them.

Clamp the two small bubbles onto your nose, and presto! You look as goofy as a clown.

EYEGLASSES

A balloon shaped into a pair of giant eyeglasses goes well with the clown nose.

Inflate a #260 balloon fully except for about two inches. Twist off bubbles 1 and 2. Loop connect bubble 2. Twist off bubbles 3 and 4, loop twisting bubble 4.

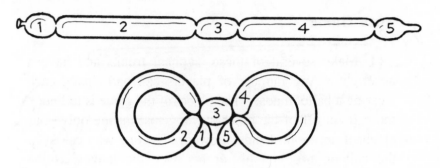

You can use this creation as a pair of eyeglasses or as handcuffs.

PIRATE SWORD

Kids love to play with swords. Here is a sword that's fun and safe. Inflate a pencil balloon fully except for about one inch. Twist off one medium bubble and one extra large bubble about 11 inches long. Twist connect points A and B. Bend bubble 3 back and through the loop of bubble 2. Bubble 2 becomes the hand guard and bubble 3 the blade.

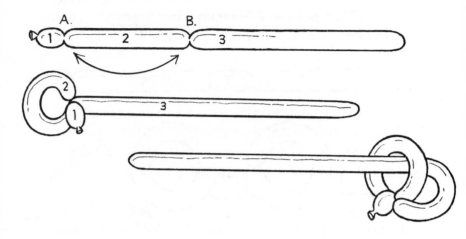

BUBBLE GUN

Here's a balloon gun that really works. The bullets are tiny balloons which you make. Let's start by making a bullet. Inflate a pencil balloon eight inches or more. Twist off a small bubble. Now insert this bubble into the balloon, as shown in the illustration.

PUSH →

Use a pin and make a hole in the balloon behind the small bubble. Let all the air out of the large balloon; the small balloon will remain inflated. Cut off the excess balloon, and your bullet is finished. The double wall makes these little bubbles very durable.

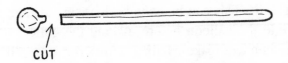

CUT

To make the gun, start by tying a knot in an uninflated balloon two inches from the nipple. Cut off the nipple end and discard. This is done merely to shorten the balloon. Inflate the balloon fully except for about a fourth of an inch, and tie it off.

Make the gun exactly the same way as the sword. Since you shortened the balloon, instead of a long sword blade you end up with a short gun barrel (see the illustration).

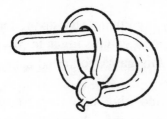

Push the bullet into the barrel of the gun. Grab the bullet with your trigger finger and thumb, and hold it until your're ready to fire. Shoot by aiming and releasing the bubble. The bullet can be harmlessly shot ten feet or more.

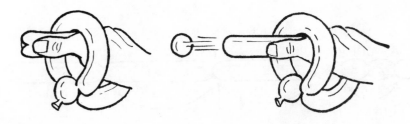

68

If you would like the bullet to go farther, add more weight to it. This can be done by inserting a small wad of paper into the balloon before making the bullet.

The gun can make exciting games for kids. Give each one a gun and some bullets and play shoot-'em-up or have a one on one shoot-out.

Form a large ring of trigger happy kids around a single brave soul and play dodgeball, using the balloon guns instead of balls. The shooter whose bullet hits the player in the center of the ring becomes the new target and must evade all flying bubbles. They'll have a gas.

FEARLESS FREDDY

Fearless Freddy Fly Fighter (try saying that real fast five times) is a fun balloon game similar to pin the tail on the donkey. To play this game you need a big, ugly fly and several fly zappers.

Where do you find a big, ugly fly? No, you don't need to look in your garbage can. You will make one out of a balloon. You will also make the fly zappers.

Let's start with the fly. Blow up a pencil balloon, leaving about an inch uninflated. Burp the balloon to soften it, then tie it off. Twist off one soft bubble (1) small to medium in size and two medium bubbles (2 and 3). Connect points A and B.

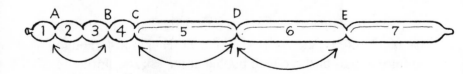

Twist off a medium to small bubble (4) and a large bubble (5). Loop twist bubble 5, connecting points C and D.

Make bubble 6 the same size as bubble 5 and loop twist it, connecting points D and E. Bubbles 5 and 6 form the fly's wings, and the remaining bubble becomes the body.

Push bubble 1 about a fourth of the way between bubbles 2 and 3. Use your marker to draw two very large eyes on bubbles 2 and 3. Draw two dots on bubble 1 for the nose. Your fly is complete.

Each fly zapper is made with one pencil balloon. Inflate the balloon fully, then release all the air leaving just enough to form a two- or three-inch bubble at the nozzle. Inflating

the balloon first makes the zapper's tail larger and easy to
see.

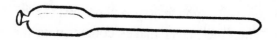

Make one fly zapper for each player and write the
player's name on the bubble. Insert a straight pin into the
nozzle of each zapper, as shown below.

You are now ready to play the game. Tape the mon-
strous fly on the wall at about shoulder level. The object
of the game is to zap (pop) the fly with the fly zapper while
blindfolded.

Each contestant in turn assumes the the role of Fearless
Freddy Fly Fighter, armed with a powerful fly zapper on a
mission to rid the house of a giant, pesty fly.

Players are led one at a time to a spot several feet in
front of the fly, and are blindfolded. Once the blindfold is

in place, the player turns around several times to get slightly dizzy, and then is pointed toward the fly. Holding up the zapper, he or she walks toward the fly and sticks the pin into the wall (you can use tape instead of a pin if desired). When the player makes contact with the wall his zapper loses its power and must remain where it landed until the game is over. Then the next player tries his skill, and so on until everyone has had a chance to be Fearless Freddy. The winner is the player whose zapper is closest to the fly, or who succeeds in popping it.

If someone pops the fly before all the players have had a turn a new fly is made and used. If two or more players happen to pop the fly, they must either share the prize or play one more time. If the fly was not destroyed, the winner (the one whose zapper was closest to the fly) has the privilege of popping the balloon without the blindfold and become the hero.

CREATIVE CLOWNING

Edited and Compiled by Bruce Fife
Foreword by Richard Snowberg
President, World Clown Association

A delightful book on the art of being a funny clown. Contains 224 large pages (8.5" x 11") with over 200 illustrations.

Some of the topics include: comedy magic • balloon sculpturing • funny juggling • balancing buffoonery • fun with puppets • clown music • mime and physical comedy • stilt walking and unicycling • clown makeup and wardrobe • developing a lovable clown personality • controlling an audience • creative use of props • how to create jokes and funny routines • how to tell jokes and be a good comedian • how to start your own birthday party business • where and how to find good paying jobs as a clown.

Available at your local bookstore or magic dealer, or you can order it directly from the publisher (price $17.95 postage paid).

BRUCE FIFE • TONY BLANCO • STEVE KISSELL
BRUCE JOHNSON • RALPH DEWEY • HAL DIAMOND
JACK WILEY • GENE LEE

Java Publishing Co.
Dept. B
6510 Lehman Drive
Colo. Spgs., CO 80918

Send a long self addressed stamped envelope for a free descriptive brochure of other books from Java Publishing Co.